Skippy's Rescue

An Easter Island Adventure

ED TREVINO

Copyright © 2019 Ed Trevino
All rights reserved
First Edition

PAGE PUBLISHING, INC.
New York, NY

First originally published by Page Publishing, Inc. 2019

ISBN 978-1-68456-017-2 (Paperback)
ISBN 978-1-68456-019-6 (Digital)

Printed in the United States of America

Introduction

We lived in a rural area, in a home where our closest neighbors were a good half mile down the road. All of our children learned to enjoy what their surroundings offered them. Acres upon acres of farmland and a large forest beyond the acres. Ed was the youngest of seven at the time, and he had plenty of time to enjoy the outdoors while his brothers and sisters were away at school. Our family dog Peanut was his closest friend. Peanut was a very smart mutt. Whenever Ed's mom was looking for Ed, all she had to do was call for Peanut to go find Ed, and a couple of minutes later they both would appear at the door.

A few years later, the family moved to a small town close by. Down the street from the family's home were a pair of German shepherd that would always bark warnings and show their canine teeth to the children when they walked past the chain-leak fence. The owner of the dogs had Beware of Dog signs posted on every corner of the fence that surrounded the home, but neither the dog's warnings nor the owners' warnings were enough to stop Ed.

My job was about a half a block away from the family's home. During lunch breaks, I would walk home to meet my wife and the children for lunch. One day as I was walking home, I heard the two shepherd's barking, when I looked toward the dogs, I saw Ed climbing the fence to be with the dogs. Before I could call out Ed's name in fear the dogs would attack him, he had already landed on the other side of the fence with the dogs. Fearing the dogs would attack Ed, I hurried to the fence, only to witness Ed standing between the ferocious dogs, petting each dog as if they were best of friends.

My wife, Angelique and I have always been the adventurous couple when it comes to vacations, whether it was the Galapàgos Islands of Ecuador, the ruins of Machu Picchu, Peru, or the ruins of Tikal, Guatemala. We were seeking adventure.

For our five-year wedding anniversary, we wanted to take another adventure vacation, but where? Angelique being the ancient history geek she is, watched a program on TV about Easter Island and told me about the moai statues on the island the next morning.

I heard about Easter Island awhile back, it may have been in grade school, or I may have watched a movie about the island years ago, but nothing was registering. Of course, when in doubt, you search the World Wide Web to find the answer.

Bingo! Kevin Costner made a movie in the '90s about Rapa Nui (Easter Island), and I remember watching a portion of the movie. Tribesmen of different clans climbing up and over lava rocks dive off a cliff into the Pacific Ocean and swim to a smaller island, collect a bird egg, secure the egg, and swim all the way back to Easter Island.

The first tribesman back to Easter Island with the egg unbroken would win, and their clan would rule the island for a year. The clan leader would be known as the "Birdman." After reading more about the island on the computer, I thought yes this would be an ideal adventure vacation for our fifth wedding anniversary.

After arriving on Easter Island, we took a cab to our motel room, though the ride was only five minutes, we did get to see some sites of the island along the way. We watched a few surfers ride the Pacific Ocean waves, seen a beautiful moai statue, and had a dog run alongside the cab as the island welcoming party. We checked in to our room and headed straight away to an ocean view restaurant we spotted along the way. It was a windy first day on the island, which made it practically impossible to sit outside and enjoy the fresh catch of the day for lunch, but we managed.

After lunch, we walked over to a few landmarks that were next to a children's playground. While reading the writing on one of the landmarks, a stray dog nuzzled up close to us. The dog was very docile and allowed us to give him a pat on the head, good boy.

We walked north along the coastline and looked at a gigantic moai statue. We thought how incredible the challenge must have been to not only carve the statue, but to transport it and erect it at this final location all by hand. While walking along the coastline, we kept running into stray dogs, all of them were very docile, a few of them were a tad timid, and none of them were the mean angry stray. Having to leave our two dogs at home, it was nice to be able to have some canine companionship. Old habits are hard to break, and when it came to stray dogs, this was one habit we both agreed we were going to keep. We decided the stray dogs on Easter Island needed to be fed and watered, just like the stray dogs of the Galapagos Islands, Cusco, Peru, and Flores, Guatemala.

We walked a short distance and found a few souvenir shops and stopped in for a peek of future purchases, but what we really wanted to locate was a food store that would have water and some hotdogs for the stray dogs. We found a small butcher shop that had some freshly made links. We purchased a few links and some bottled water and headed back to the playground. We sat and tossed pieces of the links to a few dogs, and we poured water into a paper cup for those who were thirsty. We gathered up our things and made a promise to the stray dogs that we would be back tomorrow.

Angelique arranged for us to take a tour of the moai quarry the next morning. We felt it best we get some sleep tonight so we have enough energy for the following day. The next morning, the wind had died down, but a rain cloud sat over the island and drizzled for most of the day. We took a tour bus to Rano Raraku quarry, the quarry was actually a volcanic crater that the Rapa Nui people turned into a quarry. They used the large portions of volcanic rock to make the large moai statues. In the quarry, an incomplete statue lays in the earth. The incomplete moai seems to have been abandoned. Maybe the carvers encountered inclusions of very hard rock in the material and could not finish this moai?

Ahu Tongarki

Others may be sculptures that were never intended to be separated from the rock in which they are carved. Again, some of the moai's are just above an average man's height, though moving them would not be easy, we envision the pulley system—the Rapa Nui used to move them. Then we come across moai's that are ten, fifteen, twenty-feet tall and weigh a few tons each. You begin to wonder how many villagers would it have taken to move such a massive statue.

After our tour of the quarry, our tour guide promised us the best shrimp empanada on the island. But, first we would have to go see the moai's of Ahu (shrine) Tongariki. Ahu Tongariki is the largest ahu on Easter Island. Its moai were toppled during the island's civil wars and in the twentieth-century, the ahu was swept inland by a tsunami. It has since been restored and has fifteen moai including a moai that was the heaviest ever erected on the island. Prior to getting up close to Ahu Tongariki, you come across a single moai statue which is named "The Traveling Moai" it has traveled to Japan for a world's fair, and it has also been used for walking experiments on the island itself. Ahu Tongariki is approximately one mile from Rano Raraku and Poike in the Hotu-iti area of Rapa Nui National Park. All the moai here face sunset during summer solstice.

Our last stop on this tour took us to Anakena Beach which is on the eastern side of the island. It is also where we filled our bellies with shrimp empanadas. An empanada is a stuffed bread or pastry baked or fried in many countries of Latin America and in Spain. The name comes from the Spanish verb *empanar*, meaning to wrap or coat in bread. The tour guide was correct, the empanadas were indeed fabulous. Of course, while enjoying our empanadas, some stray dogs came around looking for some scraps but also looking for a little human companionship.

After our tour, Angelique and I rested awhile in our room. When we both felt recharged enough, we decided to head to the children's playground and feed hotdogs to some stray dogs. We tossed pieces of hotdogs to a few stray dogs and even fed a couple of them out of our hand. We were amazed at the great number of strays that wandered the island and couldn't understand how come the island had so many of them? Of course, some of the dogs probably belonged to villagers' but still the number was great.

SKIPPY'S RESCUE

Puppy in gangway

We finished feeding the dogs all the hotdogs we had with us and decided to get ready for a nice dinner. As we walked back to our room, a puppy appeared from between a gangway. I stopped and snapped a picture of the cute puppy, and Angelique mentioned, "Maybe he's hungry too?"

I asked Angelique if she wanted to go and get some more hotdogs and feed the puppy? Knowing the answer would be yes, I put my camera away, and we headed back to the butcher shop. We got back to where we last saw the puppy, and the puppy had moved on.

Angelique suggested we head to the playground to see if the puppy was there. We made our way over to the playground, and sure enough there we found the puppy. We realized the puppy was a female and found her to be adorable. She had big ears that were way too big for her head and beautiful eyes. She was very shy and would not get close to us even with hotdog scraps being offered.

Angelique tossed her a piece of hotdog, then another and another, until we thought she would follow us. We found a nice quiet spot in the playground and continued offering scraps. The pup stood firm and would not get close to us, I always knew Angelique had patience (she married me), but the patience she showed this evening was truly remarkable.

Angelique lay on the ground and stretched her hand out and offered the pup more hotdog. It took the pup quite some time to realize Angelique and I meant no harm, and the pup finally succumb to her hunger and started eating the hotdog out of Angelique's hand. The pup got comfortable enough that Angelique was now sitting on the ground, feeding the pup from her hand. We both fell in love with the puppy and promised her we would be back tomorrow to feed her again.

Angelique and I went back to our room and got ready for our anniversary dinner. We picked another restaurant that overlooked the Pacific Ocean, and though the sunset and dinner were beautiful and delicious, we both couldn't help but discuss the puppy we had met earlier in the day. We made plans that evening to find a store the next morning that sold dog food and go out and feed more strays, but the real mission was to find that puppy we both fell in love with.

SKIPPY'S RESCUE

Building trust

As we sat and discussed the next day's itinerary, our server informed us of some caves on the northern portion of the island that we would enjoy exploring. Our next day on the island was set, we would find some real dog food, feed and water some strays, and then trek north to explore some caves. We toasted our anniversary and made our way back to the room for a good nights' rest.

The next morning, we got into our hiking gear and headed out to find some dog food. We came upon a *supermercado* that sold three-and-ten-pound dog food bags. We bought the three-pound bag and headed toward the children's playground, along the way we fed some stray dogs. A few of them followed us to the playground, others stayed behind. Believe it or not, a Yorkshire terrier continued to tag along with us. It is hard to believe this dog would be a stray because he was groomed so well. We knew he had to belong to someone. He wasn't after the food we poured out for the strays, he just wanted to belong. We didn't mind him tagging along, we named him Mr. Yorkie.

As we approached the playground, we spotted the little puppy from yesterday laying down next to two other dogs. As we got closer, we realized one of the other dogs could be the puppy's mother or father. *Probably mother?*

Yep, it's the puppy's mom, she had the same color and wiry terrier coat, and the other dog was also a female and had some characteristics of the puppy and the mom. Right away, I told Angelique, "I think one of them is the puppy's mom and the other looks to be an older sister from a different litter?"

Well, we were there to feed some stray dogs and so we did. There must have been a dozen or so dogs in the park looking for food. We poured out portions of dog food scattered about in the park, so a lot of dogs can eat. We also enticed the puppy and the other two females to follow us with a hotdog away from the other dogs.

It was remarkable, a full-blown dog fight didn't break out, sure we heard a few growls, but it was mainly some alpha dogs putting other dogs in their place. They all got to eat some food. We fed the three females some dog food away from the other dogs and gave them all fresh water.

There was enough food and water left over for our little Yorkie that decided to tag along, so we fed him too. After these four dogs ate, we wanted to see if they would follow us north and explore the caves with us.

SKIPPY'S RESCUE

The Hike

We got up and started walking, and sure enough, we had a pack of dogs. Before long, a beautiful black stray with beautiful eyes joined us, he had the same eyes as the little puppy, and he looked like he had some German shepherd in him which would match some of the markings of the puppy even the big German shepherd's ears matched.

The black dog reminded Angelique of her dog Zoe that passed away a few months back, so we named him Zo2. We now had a pack of five dogs that seemed to know each other from roaming the streets which made it easy for them all to tag along with us on the hike we were taking.

We managed to get all five dogs to open field on the island, and were moving along quite nicely until a few alpha dogs stopped us in our tracks. The alphas left Mr. Yorkie and Zo2 alone and concentrated on the girls, they snarled and growled at the girls and tried to pin them down. Angelique even kneed one of the dogs to get them off of the puppy's mom.

Once we were able to get the alpha dogs off the girls, we sent the girls back to the playground where we knew they would be safe. As for Mr. Yorkie and Zo2, they were willing to continue to follow us, so we began our trek to the caves. We must of walked a good ten to fifteen minutes wondering and hoping the girls made it back to the playground safely?

Then all of the sudden, from a nearby street, we see the three girls running toward us. I just couldn't give a rightful explanation of how happy Angelique and I were to see those three girls joining our pack again. The hike was on again, and our pack of five fell in line and marched on. We must of hiked a good mile more before we all needed to take a break. We found a shaded spot along a cliff wall sat and quenched our thirst.

As the humans sat out in the sun, the pack all gathered in the shade. Angelique and I sat with the pack discussing each dog. Mr. Yorkie was a character of a dog, he didn't have the "small dog syndrome," but he thought highly of himself. Zo2 would be a very loyal companion, he was always right there by your side even if a grazing horse distracted him for a few minutes, he'd returned right by your side.

SKIPPY'S RESCUE

The Girls return

When we first met the puppy, Angelique couldn't get over the big ears of the pup, she had the face of a kangaroo with big ears. With that in mind, I said, "Let's name her Skippy, like the program *Skippy the Bush Kangaroo*."

It was a cute name. Angelique and I would be able to identify the puppy with, After we leave the island, someone else will come along and rename the puppy to suit their admiration for the puppy. Until then, Skippy it is.

The other two females were inseparable, the younger female was very affectionate. She was always willing and wanting to give paw for a little human kindness. The older female was very shy, she kept her distanced, but she made up for that by her uncanniness to catch every treat thrown her way. Left, right, up, down, it didn't matter she had great mouth and eye coordination. I threw out the names FiFi and CiCi.

Angelique agreed and our pack of five was named. After the break, we gathered the pack and continued our journey to the caves.

We came to a complete stop when a farmer's fence stood in our way. Angelique and I both were bummed, we wouldn't explore some caves on this trek, but the company of the pack was well worth the trek north.

We decided to take the dogs back to the playground and let them rest. Besides, Mr. Yorkie's parents are probably looking for him. We got back to the playground without any issues from the alpha dogs, they must have been out looking for a meal when we walked beyond their territory. We left the girls at the park with some fresh water, Zo2 escorted us to our motel entrance and wandered off into the neighborhood. Mr. Yorkie found another tourist to pester.

We needed a good rest after that trek.

Mr. Yorkie

The next couple of days, we kept a schedule with the three girls and Zo2, Mr. Yorkie would appear once in a while, but our solid pack was now four. We'd feed and water the pack in the morning, go off and be tourist in the afternoon, return to the park in the early evening, and feed the foursome. It was a good feeling taking care of dogs while we missed our two back home. We didn't forget about the rest of the strays on the island, they all were fed when we got to the park, but we always managed to pull our pack away from the fray of the other strays to get some alone time with them.

Early morning, a rain cloud visit the island, it put a damper on our routine. We stayed within the motel's grounds for most the day. The motel was even showing a screening of Kevin Costner's *Rapa-Nui* movie in the dining room. Angelique and I took a pass, we decided to wait the rain out. Once the sun appeared, we were anxious to get to the playground to check on our pack.

Along the way, Zo2 appeared from under a structure, he was damp but seemed willing to join us in the sun to dry off. We found the girls in the playground area, also trying to dry off from the rain with the sun. We got the girls attention, and they all seemed happy to see us. We found a quiet spot and offered food and water to our four friends.

After getting her fill, Skippy wandered off and found a piece of plastic and turned it into a chew toy. The others took a spot in front of the bench Angelique was sitting on. I started taking some pictures of Angelique and the three strays. Again, if I didn't see it with my own eyes, I would not have believed these three dogs were actual strays. They all seemed so content, lying in front of Angelique, it was really a beautiful sight.

Then it happened, the moment I knew our Easter Island story wasn't going to end on Easter Island.

Skippy had grown tired of her new found chew toy and wanted to antagonize her elders. She tried Zo2, and he wasn't having any of it, she then tried FiFi, and FiFi got up and moved.

As she crossed Angelique's path heading to mommy, Skippy was scooped up and placed in Angelique's lap. This was the moment good intentions turned to affection. The bond at that second was sealed. The past days we had with the dogs were all because of our compassion for other beings. We would not stand idle and watch dogs go hungry and thirsty, we did what most dog lovers would do.

The Bond

As soon as Angelique picked Skippy up, I knew right then Angelique was diagraming a plan in her mind to take Skippy home with us. It is awfully hard to avoid compassion turning in to unconditional love, it happens with no warning. Whatever urged Angelique to pick Skippy up was unknown to me, but when I saw those two at peace with the act, I knew I couldn't allow thousands of miles to keep them separated. Somehow, someway, these two will have a reunion. It amazes me, how a human always seems to have that one moment with a dog that propels a canine, human friendship to an unconditional love relationship.

It happens all the time at a dog pound (probably not as often as needed) someone goes in looking to adopt a dog. They meet and greet a few dogs and bam one of those dogs, captures a heart and from that point forward, a relationship like no other is formed. I took a few more pictures, before the time came for us to head off and get ready for another nice dinner. We had two more days on the island, and I am sure some of the time we have left will be spent looking into adopting Skippy. Only time will tell.

Angelique and I talked about the possibilities of rescuing Skippy and taking her home with us. I thought the chance of that happening would be slim, but you never know till you try. The first thing we needed to do was contact the island's vet and ask questions.

Most of the next day was spent trying to locate the island's vet, we must of walked past the clinic a good four or five times and not once was the vet in. We did get to speak to the elder lady that handled the dog and cat food next door to the clinic, she informed us he is a very busy man and is rarely in his office. We told her of our desire to adopt one of the strays and take her back home with us. She marbled at our ambition and handed us a card with the vet's phone number. She said keep trying to call him and eventually, he will answer.

We stuck to our routine with the pack for the last two days, between feeding times, we revisited the souvenir shops and buried ourselves in trinkets. We had a conversation with the motel owner, and he thought it was a great gesture saving one of the island strays, but he wasn't interested in getting involved. He told us we were on the right track trying to contact the vet, only he wasn't privy to an easier way of getting a hold of the vet.

Zo2

We walked by the vet's office a few more times, sometimes on purpose, other times incidental, no matter the vet was never available.

Maybe Skippy finding a new home just isn't meant to be. Let's enjoy tomorrow with the dogs and head home. Our flight is scheduled for departure just after 1:00 p.m. tomorrow. Let's enjoy one final dinner tonight.

We had just enough time to enjoy a final breakfast and head to the children's playground for one more feeding with our pack. In my mind, I begin to think, *Who is going to save these dogs, will care for them when they need shelter, feed them when they are hungry, quench their thirst? Give them unconditional love?*

As usual, Zo2 came out from behind a structure and started nuzzling my hand to let me know he was among us. A half block down, we see our three girls in the playground, Skippy is gnawing on a dried-up palm tree branch, CiCi and FiFi have taken up residents on a knoll, enjoying the morning sun.

We lead our pack to a spot on the island that overlooks the Pacific Ocean, the water is calm and the sea birds are among us overhead. We pour out the final meal for the pack, and they all enjoy their fill. We gave them fresh water and sat in silence for a while.

"Maybe when we get home, I can start asking questions about rescuing Skippy?" Angelique said.

"That would mean you would have to come back to get her?"

"If that is what it takes to give her love, I am willing to try." Angelique bent over and picked Skippy up one last time and placed her in her lap. She gave her a loving squeeze and told Skippy, "I'm coming back to save you my Easter Island angel."

If you were to ask me, which of us two is the more determined than the other—hands down, it would be Angelique. Somehow, someway Skippy will become a United States of America canine citizen, you can mark her words. I snap a few more pictures of the two, and as I snap the last picture, I can see Angelique's heartache through my lens. This is going to be a very emotional flight home.

How I wish we could have taken a direct flight home. The more time Angelique and I had to sit and wait between flights and then being strapped in a seat for three to eight hours at a time, the more we had time to think about our Easter Island Angels. If it were up to Angelique, she would have already booked flights back to Easter Island on our way home. She was bound and determined Skippy would soon be at home with us.

Last day of vacation

We finally land in Chicago, one last car ride to our home, and we can settle back into our normal life. Thanks to our neighbor, Kathy, Nocioni, and Lobo are healthy and happy to see us. They welcome us home with open paws and facial licks.

Angelique and I take refuge on a sofa and talk about our vacation. The vacation was a huge success, we managed to meet a very nice couple from the United Kingdom, Kev and Georgie. We also managed to learn more about the Rapa Nui and moai ahu's. We enjoyed wonderful dinners, moonlit nights, the sky waltzing with stars, sounds of the ocean crashing the coastline, and the howling of stray dogs. Easter Island is a definite must-do vacation.

It's early June, and I must catch up with some spring jobs out in the yard. I informed Angelique I have to cut the grass before I go back to my job on Monday then I head out to the garage. I'll be busy for a good portion of the afternoon which gives Angelique plenty of time to start looking into rescuing Skippy.

SKIPPY'S RESCUE

I don't want to sound like a skeptic, I really do believe in miracles, but trying to rescue a dog that lives in the belly button of this great big world of ours, I just couldn't see it, especially when we just returned from this very expensive belly button!

Hours turned into days, days into weeks, before long June was nearly over. At the start of July, Angelique received an email from the CDC (Centers for Disease Controls and Prevention), in short, the CDC informed Angelique she would be allowed to rescue a dog from Easter Island.

Easter Island Angels

Angelique returned an email and thank the CDC for the offering. Angelique informed the CDC we would like to rescue three dogs from the island not just one. Why not? If you're going all the way back, we might as well try to bring all three girls back.

The CDC retorted with a stern no to Angelique's request to rescue three dogs. The CDC said we can rescue one dog only and it must be quarantine on the island for thirty days prior to coming to the United States of America. That meant we had to talk to the vet (good luck) and have someone capture Skippy for us (good luck) and quarantine her for thirty days (good luck) and then put her on four flights to get back to us (good luck).

We talked to our vet and told her of our dilemma, she informed us we could ask the CDC for permission to have Skippy vaccinated on the island and then transported home and quarantined in our home. We didn't have much to lose, Angelique got back in touch with the CDC and offered them our solution to the issues.

The CDC agreed to our proposal and was willing to have Skippy quarantined at our home. Okay, Angelique is now on a roll and if you stand in her way, you'll get bowled over.

During this time, I started posting photo shows of our trip to Easter Island. I posted one show named, Skippy with Lenny Kravitz song "Calling All Angels" as the background music. The show pretty much tells the story of Skippy, and people seemed to gravitate to the story.

I told Angelique, we would have to sit down and really come up with a plan of how we are going to afford her going back to Easter Island capture Skippy and bring her back home. Angelique said we would be able to afford the trip back, but it would really strain our bank accounts.

I told Angelique worry about booking her flights back, and I'll start a Go Fund Me account and see if some friends would like to help our cause. The deeper Angelique dug in, the more I started realizing, there could be a miracle among us.

By the end of July, all the paperwork from the CDC had arrived, Angelique nearly has flights booked, and a motel room reserved. She begins to tell me her itinerary and then informs me, I would be the one going back to Easter Island. *Oh okay, wait, what, me?*

She felt it best that I go back because I would be able to do what is needed to get the dog safely back. Angelique thought her emotional connection with Skippy would hinder the rescue. She knew I wouldn't let my love for animals interfere with doing what is best for Skippy. I had to admit she was right. Angelique also wanted to tell me, one of her friends read about our desire to rescue Skippy and saw that we now had a Go Fund Me account for the rescue.

Angelique's friend's name is Mary Lou, and she informed Angelique she would be making a large donation directly to Angelique. I knew there were angel's among us, but to donate such a large sum of money to a cause, that may or not actually happen is such a giant step in humanity—it brought me to tears.

I kept informing all my friends on Facebook and updating the Go Fund Me account our goal is within reach. Then our bubble burst, Angelique got word from the airlines she booked the return trip on, that if the air temperature is above eighty-five degrees, Skippy would not be able to fly in cargo. If that is the case, how could we get her home?

Once again, Angelique started asking questions and worked very hard to find another way around the airline gap. Angelique was informed Skippy would be able to sit in the cabin with me if only she was an ESA (Emotional Support Animal). The next question was, how do we make Skippy my ESA?

Angelique contacted a doctor on line and informed the doctor of our dilemma. The doctor informed Angelique she will have to send Angelique a questioner, and we would have to fill it out in order for her to "diagnose my condition."

We filled the form out and sent the form back to the doctor. The doctor called us and asked us one very important question, "Is Mr. Trevino emotionally attached to the dog in question?"

The truth is, Angelique is attached, I just want what's best for Angelique and Skippy. "Yes, Doctor. My husband is emotionally attached to the dog."

"I will forward you all the paperwork you will need to have the dog fly in the cabin with your husband."

Oh my, this is really going to happen.

As the days grew closer, there was a buzz going around at home and work about our attempt to rescue Skippy. My departure date was drawing nearer, and Angelique kept asking me, "Are you excited yet?"

I just kept telling her, "I will be excited when I see you and Skippy meet once again."

I was on Facebook when an instant message came through:

> I read your post to my mom and sister Pam, and we all are so amazed by your plan. I will mail a check today so you can get it by Friday. I think you said that's when you are leaving. Please send me your home address. Would like to send you a check that way. I'm so hopeful you find Skippy!
>
> Take care,
> The Winterhoff family

This is a high school classmate, that besides Facebook, we allowed many years to come between us, and yet because of our common love for animals and humanity, she and her family were willing to take a chance on our rescue. Angelique, Skippy and I will always be indebted to Mary Lou and the Winteroff family, along with the other friends that donated to Go Fund Me.

My bag is packed, I'm ready to go.

I don't want to bore you with the flights it took to get back to Easter Island. Let's just say a straight shot from Chicago to Easter Island is approximately five thousand miles. The route I took, four flights totaling nine thousand miles in twenty-three hours.

Easter Island (Spanish: Isla de Pascua) is a Chilean island in the southeastern Pacific Ocean, at the southeastern most point of the Polynesian Triangle. Easter Island is famous for its 887 extant monumental statues, called moai, created by the early Rapa Nui people. Easter Island is a special territory of Chile that was annexed in 1888. Administratively, it belongs to the Valparaíso Region, and more specifically, it is the only commune of the Province Isla de Pascua.

According to the 2012 Chilean census, the island has about 5,800 residents, of which some 60 percent are descendants of the aboriginal Rapa Nui. Easter Island was once home to lush palm forests. Over time, however, the humans who settled there depleted the island's resources, leading to wars among clans that doomed the population. The Dutch Admiral Roggeveen on board the *Arena* was the first European to visit the island on Easter Sunday, 1722. It is believed Admiral Roggeveen introduced dogs to the Rapa Nui clans, when he and his crew brought sheep to graze on the lush land of the island.

Skippy Grew

I arrived on Eastern Island Friday afternoon, the hotel was kind enough to pick me up from the airport. I was shown my room and handed the keys. I dropped my luggage, grabbed some treats, the lasso leash and walked to the park were Angelique and I always found the girls.

I made a complete circle of the park stopping short of where the girls had been bullied. I walked along the sidewalk on the east side of the park and found the girls lying in a grassy knoll. My first thought was, *Oh, Skippy you got big!*

I said my hello to the girls and made the noises I used in the past to get them to come. Not sure if they remembered me, but they were quick to follow me. I led them back to the park and began feeding them treats. CiCi is a very good catcher, I tossed her treats. FiFi with the paw sat close to me. At this point Skippy was eating out of my hand, each time she took a treat I would make her take it with the lasso leash between her and the treat. She would put her head through the lasso to take the treat of which she had no problem with, but I wanted her to feel comfortable, so I ignored lassoing her.

Once the treats started running out I knew I had to attempt to lasso her. I made my move and she protested, she protested hard after a few minutes she stopped protesting and froze. I tried giving her a treat but she wouldn't take it. This presented a huge problem. With limited time, I couldn't remove the leash and think I could try later that was not an option. I got up and tried to move her, she was grounded and had all four paws dug in and wouldn't move.

In the real world, time is an ally, and I could have sat there all day waiting for her to break, but my time was limited, and I didn't want to lose her on the first day. In my opinion, most dogs that have behavioral issues it's due to an owner not willing to take the time to work with the dog. Here, I have a dog that I am willing to work with but can't because of time constraints, I let Skippy out of the lasso, and she darted off under the jungle gym. Hope this attempt at a rescue doesn't come back to bite me.

SKIPPY'S RESCUE

Dug in protest

The girls needed some water after the treats, so I left to get some water and a pack of hotdogs. I got back to the park and the girls were there as I left them, taking shelter under a jungle gym. FiFi, as always was the first to see me and came out to greet me, CiCi and Skippy followed, though Skippy was a bit hesitate. *Damn.*

She warmed up to the hotdogs and took a few pieces from my hand, but we need to build trust again. I gave the girls plenty of water and made sure they all had their fill. As I was getting ready to leave, two police (*policia*) cars pulled up. Four *policias* got out and huddled a minute or so, I didn't think anything of it till they made a beeline my way. *Uh oh!*

One *policia* greeted me, "Hola," and asked me in Spanish what I was doing at the park.

I played dumb and asked him to speak in English because my Spanish is bad. *Not a lie.* He asked me in English what I was doing.

I told him I was on vacation, saw some dogs were hungry and thirsty, so I got them food and water. He asked me where I was from and how I had gotten to Easter Island. I told him I was from Chicago, Illinois, USA, and told him the route I took to get to Easter Island.

He then asked if I liked dogs.

Silly question, yes of course I do.

He asked if I would like to take one back to Chicago with me.

"Of course," I bit and said, "Yes."

He then stated, "Chile does not permit stray dogs to leave the island."

I asked, "Why not?"

He said, he doesn't know exactly, but it's not permitted. All four *policias* said their goodbyes and left.

I got up and walked to the other side of the park to call Angelique. I told her what had just happen. I believe a visitor or an islander may have called the police when they witnessed me trying to capture Skippy. This rescue got off on the wrong foot, I just hope I (we) have better luck tomorrow.

I told Angelique I was going to hang up and walk past the *policia* and ask if there was any way I could rescue one of the dogs of Easter Island. I knew if I got up and started walking toward the police, the girls would follow me. I will walk pass the four *policias* and there, I would ask my follow-up question. "Why wouldn't Chile allow stray dogs to be saved?"

To my surprise, one of the *policias* asked me if I really wanted one of the dogs.

"Of course." I bit again and said, "Yes."

He told me I would have to go see the vet and ask him to help me.

Wow, did not see that one coming!

I walked another half block, and the girls followed me. I was heading into an alpha territory, so I begged the girls to stay. In order for these girls to remain safe on the island, they have to be able to respect the boundaries the alpha dogs set for them. On my way back to the hotel, I stopped by the church for a little intervention. Afterwards, I grabbed a bite to eat and headed to the hotel, I was very tired, and needed a good night sleep. Only I didn't sleep well, because both my legs were cramping up bad. Go figure so concerned about the girls being hydrated, I forgot about myself.

Angelique and I noticed a couple of stray dogs on the grounds of the airport on our vacation to Easter Island in May of 2015.

One a young golden retriever and the other a mix breed of labrador/German Shepherd. I find it odd that a purebred would be presented as a stray on the island. In the United States, you don't see many purebreds running the streets as a stray, and they are usually given up for adoption at the shelters.

I'm willing to guess, the most common reason given as to why a dog is given up for adoption or even kicked out of a home to become a stray is behavior issues which in my eyes is not the fault of the dog. It goes back to what I was saying earlier about "time." Some dog owners have the mindset of, I gave this dog a home, now she has to acclimate herself to my lifestyle.

Just like a child, you have to give time for learning. Some make feeble attempts of basic obedience training, sit, lay, stay, and if the dog does not cooperate, the owner is quick to give up. I would compare raising a puppy to raising a child in some aspects. You don't throw your hands up, giving the "I give up" sign when a child is stuck reading a word. You find inventive ways for that child to learn. Puppy training is the same thought pattern. An owner should immerse themselves into the training method they choose. I personally do not use modern methods (e-collar) or conventional methods (clicker), I use voice and hand signals simultaneously. A well-behaved dog should know how to sit (one finger up), lay (palm facing down), and stay (palm up facing dog), of course, other simple word commands and sounds are also used "leave it," "hup," finger snap. A person could buy all kinds of training aids to help with raising a pup, but if they don't have the time to devout to the animal, then the animal is better off finding another owner. I imagine that is why we are seeing stray purebreds here, the original owners have no time for the dog.

Saturday and unfortunately, it has been raining all morning. Hoping the weather breaks soon, I need to get over to the vet and go see the girls. It's 2:00 p.m. and its' still raining, I have to get out and get some things done. I headed over to the vet's office and would you know it, it's closed.

When Angelique and I were here on vacation, we stopped by the vet office quite a few times and never got a chance to talk to him. I know he's the only vet, but c'mon he has to be in the office at some point. I took the time to walk down to the park, all three were huddling in the park under the jungle gym slide. Since I didn't have food, they weren't willing to come out; it's understandable staying warm and dry is worth more than a pat on the head.

I talked to Angelique this morning, and she understood the chances of Skippy actually coming home with me are slim, mainly after yesterday's fiasco with the lasso leash. We are thinking maybe I should turn my attention toward FiFi. After all, she seems to be more receptive to humans. FiFi, looks to be two to three years old and has a heart of gold. Surely, FiFi has learned how to assimilate herself around humans. If this rain ever lets up, I could head back to the park to feed and water the girls. I also want to attempt to pick FiFi up and see how she reacts. If I am successful, and she is willing, she might be the girl I bring home. But first things first, I have to get some water for myself, it's winter here, but it ain't no Chicago winter. Another two liter of water (*sin gas*) please. It's 5:00 p.m. and it has finally stopped raining, I'm headed out to find the girls. I have the puppy food Angelique packed for Skippy, some treats, and water.

I found Skippy lying in the grass all alone, no sign of CiCi or FiFi. I fed Skippy the puppy food. She was shaking from the rain but still willing to eat. She wouldn't let me close to her, and I was truly hurt but understood. I started singing Lenny Kravitz's "Calling All Angels" to myself: "Calling all angels / I need you near the ground. / I miss you dearly / Can you hear me on your cloud? / All my life / I have been waiting for someone to love. / All my life / I have been waiting for someone to love."

My mind just keeps rewinding the photo show I made for Angelique and the dogs when we first came to this island, and the picture of Angelique holding Skippy is ingrained in my mind. I have to figure out a way of reuniting these two. After she finished eating, Skippy walked away to lie back down on the grass. As she was walking away, I noticed she was limping a little. So many of these dogs are hit by cars, scooters, and motorcycles and suffer injuries that never heal properly or even looked at for that matter. I am willing to guess most of the incidents are related to how the locals drive. One of the reasons why Angelique and I were willing to go to this extreme is because we are the United States breed, if an animal is hurt or needs help, we charge to the rescue, it's bred in us. It's the compassion we feel in our hearts. I left Skippy and went to the *supermercado* for a bag of dog food. So many strays and not enough humans caring for them.

The owner of the hotel I am staying at stated the dogs are a big problem. I told him the dogs aren't the problem, the humans are the problem. He looked at me with a startled look and said, "The dogs eat my chickens!"

"What would you eat if no one fed or cared for you?"

I told him the solution is simple, capture the strays, spay and neuter them all, and eventually the "problem" goes away. I told him the islanders need to do the right thing if they don't, their problem will grow instead of going away.

I once watched a program of a person that needed help with the increasing amount of stray cats at the home. The individual that came to help her asked her, "Are any of the cats [fixed]?"

The person said no because the person could not afford to feed the cats and fix the cats at the same time.

The helper told the person, it was a wonderful thing the person was doing—caring for the cats. But that eventually the cats would become too much to handle and more than likely, they would all be euthanized.

The person said, "That would be terrible and I wouldn't want that to happen."

The helper put the person-in-contact with a feline outreach program and gradually, all the stray cats were fixed. Years later, the cat population at the homestead became more manageable for the person and no unwanted litters were born.

I got back to the park and fed some fifteen dogs with a three-pound bag of food. Only one fight broke out, but I squashed it rather quickly. I did not see CiCi or FiFi, and Skippy stayed in her grassy knoll.

It's getting close to the end of another day, I don't like to quit on things I start. I may procrastinate, but I eventually get it done. My time here is limited and each close of another day widens the miles between Skippy and our home. I am starting to feel the pressure of this task, and I am starting to hurt for Angelique and all the friends, and family members that have helped me get to this point. Angelique packed a chew toy for Skippy. Hopefully, tomorrow she will be willing to play. As for now, it's time to get another bottle of water (*sin gas*). I checked the documents from the CDC, unfortunately, the description clearly states one six- to nine-month-old female. FiFi has had at least one litter of puppies, and she surely does not look six to nine months of age.

Sunday morning and church bells are ringing, let's hope God bless us with some success today. It stormed hard last night and it is still drizzling, I am hungry and long for a cup of regular joe. I have to get up and out to get things done. My plan is to get another bag of dog food and water, feed and water some island dogs, find the girls, feed and water them, and go for a hike. If I wear Skippy down, maybe she would be more receptive to me. It's so sad I can't find a cup of plain old joe, latte or expresso, no how about just plain coffee.

Positive thoughts, positive thoughts, find the girls, feed them, and get our hike on. I hope Skippy will be more incline to allow me to be close to her today. I brought a chew toy. I just need Skippy to rough house a bit with me.

I found the girls in the park, I can see our three furry friends off in the distance. I make the sounds they recognize as me, and right away, FiFi's head pops up, spots me, and makes a dash to me followed by CiCi and Skippy. I pour the girls some chow and right away other island dogs want to be fed. I keep them at bay by pouring some more chow separate from the girls.

Once the girls are done, I give them a whiff of a single hotdog I brought along, and I lead them away from the other dogs. I need time to work with Skippy and try to earn her trust again, the other strays would just interfere with that. I tossed a piece of hotdog to

CiCi and FiFi who gives me paw, and Skippy cautiously takes some hotdog from my hand. When there is no more hotdog I poured some water, and CiCi begins to drink while FiFi is still giving paw. I pulled out the chew toy and offered it to Skippy, she softly took it in her mouth while I was still holding on to it. I wiggle it around as to play, but she didn't react. Once I let go, she took the chew toy to a knoll and started chewing. That's okay as long as she took it, and she enjoys the gesture. It's a building block, I have to gain her trust again. In order to be a successful dog owner, a person must be willing to build a good solid foundation to build up from. Again, with different circumstances, I would not have risked losing Skippy's trust the very first day, it was a calculated risk that I hope doesn't come back to bite me.

I talked more with the owner of the motel this morning, and he offered to help me meet with the vet on Monday morning. My time on the island is vanishing, and I will try anything to get this dog back to United States at this point. I took the girls on a hike, CiCi and Skippy chased a grazing horse, and FiFi kept wanting to give me paw. Every time I reach into my camera case, there is FiFi giving paw.

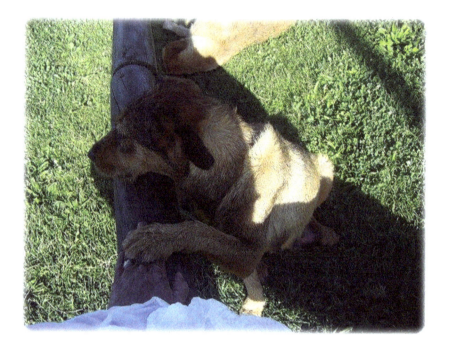

Power of the Paw

    We ended the hike at the park, and we took a siesta by the ocean. A mother and daughter stopped by and poured some food out. I made a polite mention that I had just fed them and exercised them, they could use some of your water instead of the food. They poured the food anyway. I didn't want to disturb their moment so I walked away. The girls sniffed the food and started following me. I heard the mother say how rude in Spanish as I was walking away, I stopped and told her, "They ate and just got back from a hike. They need water, and I don't have anymore."

    We walked along the sidewalk by the street and all three girls made a dash to a puddle of rain water to quench their thirst. They could have had clean fresh water if only. We found a quiet spot and relaxed a bit. The mother and daughter made their rounds with their food and stopped by us. The mother asked if the girls were mine, and I said, "No, I'm a visitor like you just trying to do the right thing."

    I didn't mean to offend anyone, but I'd just spent the last two and a half hours with the girls. I knew what they needed. Hopefully tomorrow, the vet will be able to help us get Skippy or even another terrier pup to go with me. I have to look at big pictures and somehow, someway, I'm bringing home an angel—be it Skippy or one of the other angels.

As the days go by, I have been telling Angelique what has been happening, and I told her I'm not sure I could pull this off. I just want her to know there is a chance the Skippy mission could fail. Even best-laid plans fail, and this plan is on a wing and a prayer. The girls and I ended up in an area that has a quick drop-off, so when the time is right, I could make my escape without them following me. They are safer staying away from the cars and enduro cycles. I really needed to find something to eat. I grabbed a *pollo y queso* empanada and a soda at the bakery next to the *supermercado*. After lunch, I stopped by the *supermercado* (which is smaller than a 7-Eleven), got another bag of chow and headed to the room for some rest. I'll go back to the park and feed the girls and others for dinner in a few hours.

Took the hike back to the park to feed and water the girls after my nap. Of course, when your existence is literally the circumference of a children's corner park, you won't be hard to find. I spotted FiFi and called her over to the dinner table, and she came running followed by the other two. I spread some food and put a bowl of water out and sat down to watch over them.

A couple of young ladies were watching us, and they came over to talk. They asked if I spoke Spanish, I told them, "Yes, but not well."

Luckily, one of them was fluent in English. She asked if the girls were my dogs, and I told her, "No, just some strays that I'm helping while I am here."

I told her my wife and I would like to take that one home as I pointed to Skippy. She said that would be great, she doesn't like to see so many strays and that it was like that in Santiago, Chile. I told her it's like this in many parts of the world. I told her they need to develop a program and start spaying and neutering the dogs.

She agreed.

I asked her where she learned to speak English so well. She said she is in college in Rochester, New York.

I asked her what she was studying, and she said, "Political science."

I told her, "Great! When you become president of Chile, you can fix the problem."

She smiled and said, "When I become president, I'll send for you and your wife to help fix the problem."

I left the girls with the young ladies in the park relaxing on their knoll. I stopped by the soccer field and watched the home team lose a heartbreaker, 3–9.

It's Sunday evening, and I have one more day to do what I came here to do, and I'm not sure I could pull this off. I'm pretty sure Skippy is destined to remain on Easter Island and continue being the angel she has become. Unless, of course, a miracle is bestowed upon us. I got back to the hotel, and the owner invited me to join him and a friend. They are cooking snapper and octopus on an open fire. One last good meal before I leave, *Okay. I'll bite.*

Monday morning, today is my final chance to get Skippy home, so many things have to go right for this to work, and I am yet to talk to the vet—strike ONE.

Last night, the owner of the hotel said he would help me with the vet and get Skippy. Of course, he said that half way through his second bottle of merlot. Surely he felt like superman at that moment. I had to get going with or without Matio (hotel owner).

I took a walk by the vet's office, and the lady said he should be in within the hour. So many times Angelique and I heard the same line when she was here, and we were inquiring about the strays. Even when we returned to United States, Angelique was persistent and would not give up trying to contact the vet.

I made my way to the park, the girls were in the usual area and came to me when I called them. I poured the girls breakfast, set a bowl of water up for them, and sat in silence watching my time with them dwindle. And as I contemplated the events of the time spent trying to get Skippy back to the states, I couldn't help but feel defeated. FiFi came to me and gave me her paw, she must of sense my sadness when I wasn't so receptive to her paw. She knew something was hurting me and she backed off. The tears of pain started flowing and there was no stopping them. I didn't want to be on the island any longer, let alone the park with the girls, so I got up and walked away without a goodbye. The girls must of sense my sadness because they did not try to follow me out of the park.

Mid-Monday morning and it's time to start packing for home.

A lot has happened since last I opened this journal. The owner of this hotel, Matio, of which I owe a ton of gratitude to has helped me all day long.

1. He help me finally get a hold of the vet (he does exist) and told the vet what I am attempting to do.
2. The vet informed us we had to get permission from the mayor of Easter Island to borrow a crate. The mayor agreed to allow me to borrow a crate for Skippy.
3. Matio drove me to LAN Airline to give them the dimension of the crate.
4. Matio drove me to the vet's house to get the crate.
5. Drove me to the park to "kidnap" Skippy.

His name is Matio, and I will always consider him my friend. Yes, Skippy is with me and we are waiting to see the vet, she needs to get her vaccine shots. I don't know if it's possible to mix emotions, but I was definitely welling up tears of sadness with tears of joy.

We bought some over-the-counter doggy downers for the flight home, but since the vet said he would give me something to sedate Skippy with, I thought it best to use one when I had to get her. I greeted the girls like I always do, they all came running, and I poured food and water and gave Skippy her special treat.

I didn't know if the treat would work sooner or later, I just knew I didn't have time to wait to find out. Time is definitely against me. I brought the lasso leash, and this time the plan was to slip the leash around her neck while I am scooping her up. She let me pet her head a few times with my empty hand, then I started in on both ears with both hands. Before she knew it the leash was around her, and I was scooping her up. I didn't have time to think, everything just kind of sped up for me. Before I knew it, I was half way across the park with Skippy, calling out to Matio to open the passenger door. I climbed into his SUV with Skippy on my lap. I turned to grab the door handle to close the door. As I did, I glanced out the window, FiFi had followed me to the SUV and had a paw up, as to say, take me too.

I quickly turned away and held my breath, I knew this would be the last time I see FiFi and CiCi, and it hurt so bad. It breaks my heart to have to choose one of these girls over the other two. I know taking the puppy was the right thing to do, less likely chance of having a variety of diseases. In the coming days, weeks, months, my heart will sink every time I think back to this moment. CiCi and FiFi deserve more in life. They have given so much of themselves to the visitors of this island. They, along with the other stray dogs, are constantly putting smiles on people's faces. Surely I am not the only visitor FiFi has given paw to.

Rescued first bath

Matio got us to the hotel room, and I quickly went to my room to prepare Skippy for her freedom flight. I asked Angelique to pack some Dawn soap because I knew she would have to have a flea bath once in the room. Good, now someone else can feel the effects of a cold shower. I got her in the shower stall, turn on low water pressure to soak her, and at this time, I'd have to say she is quite the trooper. Her first bath was probably better than half of the domesticated dogs in the world one hundredth bath. So good, she only objected when I turned the pressure up a bit to rinse her, and she did not like the towel dry. It's close to nine at night, and Matio just stopped by and told me the vet will be here around ten (which means closer to eleven island time). In all of today's events, I only failed to do two things—eat and drink water, and I want and need both right now.

I'm lying in bed, and Skippy is right next to me. We are waiting on the vet to arrive. She is slowly warming up to me and has moved a bit closer. The vet arrived at 10:20 p.m., I moved Skippy to the end of the bed and there she got her "freedom" shots. I thank the vet for coming so late, and he said, "I should thank you for saving this dog's life, the stray dogs on this island live a very sad life and it's good to see one of them now has a chance at a good life."

"She will be very happy in America." I shook his hand and promised him. "Skippy will live a good life. For me to come all the way back to rescue a dog I wasn't sure would be alive, let alone able to rescue."

He did not doubt my words. We shook hands again and thanked each other again, and threw in a bro hug for good measure.

The vet told me to stop by the office in the morning, and he would have the paperwork ready for me.

I said, "See you in the morning."

As we walked to the door, I let the vet out and closed the door behind him and then it occurred to me, Skippy needs a bigger crate. I walked back over to Skippy and told her, "Welcome to the family. It's time to go home."

Comfy bed

Is it too soon to exhale? I have had a very emotional day filled with a lot of highs and lows and trying to describe them, I wouldn't be able to give it justice. It's lights-out time, tomorrow is another busy day, I have to pick up Skippy's paper work, two sedatives, and exchange the crate the mayor loaned me—it's way too small (I hope LAN does not give me crap for the crate not fitting the dimensions we gave them earlier).

I finally caught a night that I could sleep well. I didn't have to worry about all the what ifs. I have what I came here for lying next to me, and I'm never letting go. I awoke in the middle of the night with Skippy actually moving herself closer to me. It was my first awe moment with her, it put a smile on my weary face. I think Angelique is trying and succeeding in driving me insane. Some of you may know how we came about Lobo, our spitz mix rescue. If not, I'll recap for you.

It was a cold March Saturday morning, and I was on the computer checking local news. Angelique walked into the room and told me she had a weird dream. I asked her what the dream was about. She said she dreamt that we saved a white dog. I told her, "Odd, I just read a story about ninety-two dogs that were being hoarded by a lady and some of the dogs are at Lake County shelter." Then I asked her if she wants to go look.

She said, "Why not."

We looked at all the dogs and not one of them was white. Angelique asked if there was a white one in the bunch, and the attendant said actually there is a white puppy, but he's in bad shape.

I asked, "How bad shape? Heartworm, defects?"

She said, "No, he checks out fine physically, but he's just really, really dramatized and has absolutely no social skills."

We asked to see him.

When we got to the holding area, we saw him in the back of a large cage, cowering in the corner. I went inside the kennel against the wishes of the shelter employee. He really was in bad shape, he couldn't even look at me to take a treat out of my hand, he smelled it and shied away.

I told her, "We could help, can we take him now?"

She said, "No, he is not ready."

I told her, "We are, and we will take him now."

She talked to the director and within forty-five minutes, the puppy was on his way home. We took the puppy home with us and began the process of rehabilitating him. The second day with us, the puppy, (Lobo) got spooked and escaped from his collar. I had our other two dogs with me, Zoe and Noci, and could not go after Lobo. I took the dog's home and went on a search for Lobo.

When Angelique got home from work, Angelique and I continued the search for Lobo all through the night. The very next day, I was to fly out to California with my Father to bury his sister. For four days, Angelique searched for Lobo and didn't have success. I had friends from Facebook helping us find Lobo. He was spotted a few times, even came to our backyard but could not be caught.

The shelter and Angelique set up a dog trap on the back deck of a neighbor's home. The neighbor fed Lobo some stew, and the shelter felt that would be the best place to catch Lobo. We did not have any success with catching Lobo the first night. On the second night, I was due home. When I got home, Angelique was in tears, Lobo is still out all alone in the bitter cold. I told her to get her gear on and let's go get Lobo.

As we drove to our neighbor's home, on the other side of the lake, Angelique kept asking, "Do you really think Lobo is in the cage?"

I told her, "Yes, he is in the cage."

At this point, I left it all up to God. When we got to the neighbor's home and peeked inside the cage, we could see a little white ball curled up in the corner of the cage. Finally, after five bitter cold lonely nights, Lobo was coming home.

Lobo

I put a front-loop walking harness on Skippy along with a martin collar. I clipped both to her leash. I was making sure, there would be no way of her getting loose. Right now, I could use the help of my boy, Nocioni (named after a basketball player Andres Nocioni), (Noci), Skippy will not walk with me.

We had the same problem with Lobo, but Noci solved that in a few minutes and had him walking around the yard on a leash. The good thing is, I am not on time restraints any longer. I'm just going to leave the gear on her and let her get used to it. We can start adjusting when we get home.

The next morning, I had to get up early and get the crate over to the doctor, so he could exchange it. I walked the one-eighth mile with the crate to the vet's office and started waiting. It's Tuesday morning, and I have to be at the airport at 11:30 a.m. to catch my 1:30 p.m. flight.

Finally, the vet arrives, and I tell him my dilemma, "The crate is too small, she will not be able to stand or turn around in the crate and that is a requirement when transporting dogs in cargo."

His assistant said, "We do not have a spare."

I told her, "I'm not taking Skippy in such a small crate."

The vet had a stern look in his eye and was adamant about not having another crate.

Then I said the magic words, "If you can't give me a larger crate, then I will have to leave her. There is no way I am going to have her suffer in a small crate."

He finally gave in and gave me a larger crate. He also said the office does not have a printer, and I would have to get a USB drive.

Wait what?

The assistant asked me if I needed a taxi to go back to the hotel, and I said sure. An SUV taxi came by, and I loaded the crate and left with the taxi. In the short time together, the taxi driver managed to tell me about his four dogs, and I told him Skippy's story.

We got to the hotel, and I asked, "How much?"

The taxi driver said, "Nada, tu e Skippy vaya con Dios." Nothing, you and Skippy go with God.

When I got back to the room, I got what I expected, Skippy had to go and go she did. I find it hard to blame any dog for improper waste management, especially if they have to "live" around our schedule. She really is liking the comfy bed as opposed to a sidewalk or a grassy knoll. This time, we are spending together takes me back to my life with my number one dog a cocker spaniel named,

Bubbs. I used to keep a journal when I had my "BUBBS" (Bear, cUbs, Blackhawks, Bulls, Sox).

Bubbs and I really moved about the country. I bought him in Florida, and at one time or another, we lived in Illinois, Tennessee, North Carolina, and Texas. He was a great friend to have for close to sixteen years. Having Skippy in my room reminds me of the days Bubbs and I stayed in Fort Stockton, Texas, for a year. A town of ten thousand, and we were just passing through.

We lived in a motel that allowed me to keep Bubbs in the room while I worked a labor job, roofing the local high school. Bubbs and I moved back home to Lansing in '98. On our last day together, Bubbs gave me his paw as to say, goodbye, my friend.

I think Bubbs is the reason why I always make a fuss about FiFi giving me her paw. That last gesture of Bubbs was the reason why Noci, our springer spaniel came into our life. Angelique and I stopped by Alsip Nursery one day looking for some lawn furniture. I went over to the puppy section and there was Noci, liver-white without a lot of spots, just what I have been looking for, for six or seven years since Bubbs passed. It might be time for a new boy.

I had him in the playpen with me, Angelique said to find her when I was done, so I played awhile with Noci and just when I was ready to put him back, he stopped in front of me and gave me a paw. I melted...and the rest is history. (Yes, I know some "nursery's" have been known to sell puppy-mill dogs,) but how can I resist the sign of the paw?

Nocioni, wore a collar around his neck, not to restrain him but to identify him. Noci was always a free thinking dog. If a sighting, scent or noise peaked his interest in the woods he was always free to investigate. Knowing full well Noci would return to us, because we were family and with us Noci called home. I still remember the first time I realized Noci had a thought pattern to life; he was just over one year old. Zoe, Noci and I were resting on a park bench watching a football team practice. Zoe was to my right and Noci to my left. Though a leash was hooked onto their collars, the leashes were out of my hand and laid on their backs. As we sat there together, me watching practice, Noci and Zoe patiently waiting for our journey home to begin. A squirrel wondered over to where we were relaxing. Inquisitively the squirrel's nose leads him to Noci. The squirrel was close enough to Noci, that a simple chomp of Noci's jaw would have put three quarters of the squirrel in his mouth, but Noci just laid there with his head up allowing another being to investigate his scent. The squirrel circled around Noci, taking in every scent, and Noci allowed it. Once the squirrel was satisfied he scampered off towards the tree line. At this time I started to reach for Noci's leash, because I thought he would give chase. But, he didn't, Noci turned and looked up at me and with his eyes as to ask, "What the heck was that all about?"

Throughout the years together, we developed our own form of communication. I used my voice and hand signals, Noci used his bark, eyes and brows. Mom always got a kick out of our arguments, when I would say no; Noci would always have a retort with an array of barks, pleading his case. If mom were a judge, she'd surely side with Noci in any of our arguments. Noci learned to use his beautiful eyes to his advantage, I don't know of one human who would be able to resist those eyes. Mom always said they were human eyes, I tend to agree.

In order to have more people enjoy Noci's company we enrolled Noci in a Therapy dog program. He passed with flying colors; in fact Noci was one of the better pupils in class. Noci was always on point when it came time for him to demonstrate his abilities. I remember one day in class, the teacher wanted to show us handlers a few things we might want to try, to get the people we were meeting to participate. She brought out a limbo stick and she and another trainer held the stick, we had to teach Noci and the other dogs how to jump over the stick. The first three times were a breeze for Noci each time the stick was raised Noci cleared it with ease. On the fourth attempt I asked Noci to add a little laughter to the exercise. I placed Noci in front of the stick, just like before, but this time when I dropped Noci's leash and went to the opposite side I put one finger up and Noci sat, I put my palm facing down and Noci laid down. I asked Noci to "army crawl" and he army crawled under the stick to where I was standing. Noci sat up to laughter, cheers, bravos and barks from the class. We proceeded to find a few places that would allow us to visit with the residents. Noci was always a star when we visited the residents and staffs. Most couldn't get over how beautiful Noci was, and the comments about his eyes were endless. With others Noci brought back memories of their younger years, when they had the same breed of dog. There were nights when we were asked to stay a little beyond visiting hours, because we had not finished visiting all of Noci's friends. One particular night stands out in my mind. We had just finished visiting on the first floor and headed up to the second floor on the elevator. As we got off the elevator and turned the corner, Noci made a sudden stop. I gave a little tug on his leash and with all his might on the slippery polished floor he stood firm. I looked back and Noci had stopped by an elder lady sitting in a wheelchair being ignored by all the people around her including myself. I went back to where Noci stopped, and I said hello to the lady, her voice was barely audible but she responded with a hello. I noticed she had tears running down her cheeks and I asked her if she would like some company. Before she could respond, Noci gently placed a paw on her lap. She grabbed for his paw and Noci allowed her to pet and rubbed on his paw. I personally do not know of too many dogs that would allow their family let alone a stranger hold on to a paw longer than a handshake. But, from a very young age Noci craved for his paws to be rubbed and massaged. Eventually the lady asked for more of Noci and asked for Noci's other paw too. I thought Noci's weight might hurt her so I was going to say no to that request, but Noci and she had their own ideas. Noci gently placed his second paw on her lap and allowed this stranger to take all the loving she needed from him. She whispered to me, she had a Springer Spaniel when she was young with the same markings and color. She told me, "Lady" was the best dog she ever owned. I had to chuckle and told her, I don't own Noci. He is a free thinking dog, and that will never ever change.

SKIPPY'S RESCUE

Nocioni 2005 – 2016

After I cleaned Skippy's mess, I stepped outside to talk to Matio. I told him, "I need to find a computer store and buy a pin drive. Did the island have such a store?"

He said, "There was a store on the main street." Then asked me if I wanted to use his SUV.

Of course I did, time is getting short on me. It's already 11:00 a.m., and I have to get to the airport. Mindful of the strays on the street, I drive erratically safe. I found the computer store, went inside, and I asked the man at the counter if he had a pin drive. He said yes and grabbed one from under the counter. He began to explain the gigabyte's and other things to me, but all I was interested in was how much.

Finally, he said seventy dollars. I'm no computer guy but a 64 gigabyte's pin drive for seventy bucks seems steep. Who cares, I bought it and went back to the vet's office and no vet. He did leave a note saying he'd be back at 11:30 a.m.

I went back to the room to pick Matio, Skippy, and my gear up, and we all turned around and headed back to the vet. Right before we left Matio's place, I reached in my pocket and pulled out a one-hundred-dollar bill and handed it to Matio.

He asked. "What it is for?"

I told him, "For helping me get this dog."

We get back to the vet's office, and he still isn't back. It's now 11:45 a.m. and the rush of events is starting to get to me. Matio asked the lady in the feed store where the vet was.

She said he was doing his weekly radio show and he will be back soon.

Five minutes later, Matio said he's going to the radio station and dragging the vet back. Not two minutes after Matio left, the vet and his assistant pulled up. We rush to put the medical information on the pin drive and then the vet gave me the sedatives and the instructions on how to give them orally. As I walked out of the office, Matio pulled up. I got in and we were off to the airport.

We arrived at the airport right about noon. Not too many people here, must not be a full flight. I gave Skippy her first sedative and started praying I wouldn't have a problem with the bigger crate. LAN Airline request any added freight to be confirmed forty-eight hours in advance. About forty-eight hours ago, I was resigned to going home alone. I didn't get the measurements to the airline till ten minutes before closing Monday afternoon and that was for the smaller crate. We are going to find out real soon if Skippy is going on to America with me. I gave the service desk the pin drive and they made copies for me. They asked me to put the crate on the scale and they weighed it. The clerk asked a baggage handler to start securing the crate and told me it would cost ninety-five dollars. HOTDOG!

As I was walking the tarmac to the plane, I can see they were still loading cargo onto the plane. I started walking up the stairs and turned and watched Skippy go up her ramp. The flight is scheduled to leave at 1:30 p.m. and landing in Santiago at 8:10 p.m. Prepare for takeoff, we are coming home.

I am sitting in my seat, and I feel as if I am having and out of body experience. I am picturing Angelique and myself with Noci, Lobo, and now Skippy walking our favorite trails in the Smokies. I can see the dogs cohabiting easily. With Noci's previous surgeries and his age creeping up on him, Lobo is going to need a playmate to run with, and Skippy will be a willing participant. I can now see the moment Angelique and Skippy bonded, over and over and over. This adventure will surely bring us all closer together. It's time to get some rest, we have a very long journey ahead of us. The flight for Bogota doesn't leave Santiago till 11:40 p.m.—the wait between flights—I surely do not look forward to.

We landed in Santiago on time. I made my way to baggage claim to get Skippy. I hope she's doing okay with the sedatives. The vet gave me a can of soft dog food to feed her once we landed in Santiago. He did not want me to feed her a lot, just enough to keep her going. It was a rather large can, and I did not want (need) an incident on the plane, so I listened to the vet and only fed Skippy a little. I wanted to make sure she was secure in the crate I opted to leave the ty-raps on and feed Skippy through the gate opening.

After I fed Skippy, I made my way to the pizza restaurant for a slice of pizza. This is one of the times I wished I wasn't raised in the "Pizza Capital" of the world. Nobody makes pizza like a Chicago pizza joint, nobody! I was under the impression I would have to pay another ninety-five-dollar ticket for Skippy when I checked her in at Santiago. The ticket agent added another ID number to Skippy's crate and said, "Gracias Senor Trevino."

"Winning!"

The waiting through all the connection flights has become the hardest part of this journey. It gives me time to reflect back on the emotional rollercoaster I have been on these five days. The days leading up to this rescue Angelique would ask me if I was getting excited. I kept saying no, not yet. You couldn't imagine the realistic dreams and even thoughts I was having days prior to departure. Everything from first seeing the girls, to giving Skippy a bath, to saying goodbye to FiFi and CiCi, so on and so on. It all seemed so real, I thought about the word failure many times the days prior to departure.

How can I let Angelique and Skippy down? These two had a bond that was only broken by miles and it was up to me I had to make the image I see in my head of these two physically touch and bonding again a reality. They say God doesn't give you more than he thinks you can handle, the trials and tribulations of life is a daily test. God fills our heart with all sorts of emotions, some good and some bad. It's up to us to discard the bad, we have to make room for more good to come from God.

I think the greatest gift God gave his children is compassion. We have the ability of showing sympathetic pity and concern for the sufferings or misfortunes of others. That's a very powerful gift if we use it in our daily lives. You don't pick and choose the good you do in daily life—you make compassion habitual in daily life—therefore, when an action is positive it propels a positive "reaction" forward. I hope by my actions going forward with Skippy are well received and do not encounter any bad. If this rescue would have gone wrong (it's not over) actually, it still can go wrong. If there is failure in the end, God, Angelique and the rest of you will know I walked miles with the burden of one animal's life on my back and through all the trials and tribulations of these days, I held on because of the belief you all had in me. Good is a powerful tool.

It is now 11:50 p.m., and I am about to board for Bogota, Columbia, this is the second leg of this four-legged race home. We will land in Bogota around 7:00 a.m. I think I'll make myself comfortable, put *Lord of the Rings: The Two Towers* on and fall asleep watching it. The most interesting part of this journey begins in Bogota. I wanted to crate Skippy with a sedative to give her time to adjust. A lot has happen in her life the past twenty-four hours and even more adjustments to come. These next two legs of the journey, Skippy will be in the cabin with me, she will be my Emotional Support Animal in training, and she will be on sedatives but only half a dosage this time. I am so exhausted, but I can see the finish line off in the distance, it's going to be a great photo finish.

SKIPPY'S RESCUE

We land in Bogota in fifteen minutes, starting to wish I had a second set of hands on this journey, namely, Angelique's hands. Since we are now officially out of the arms of Chile, we have become fair game to the world. We took a stray from the "Bellybutton of the world" and now plan to make "The melting pot of the world" its new home. First things first, I need to get Skippy from cargo claim and then we make our way over to immigration. This is usually a snap your finger, done routine, but with Skippy different sets of circumstances lurk.

Pretty impressive, I only had to bribe the Columbian government fifty bucks to get Skippy on to the next leg of the journey USA. I was informed by an officer I had to go inside an office to get consent from a government worker to allow Skippy to step on Columbia's soil. I sat in the office and pulled out my CDC paperwork for Skippy from the USA. Besides, Skippy being closer to one year of age than the six months the paper says, everything else is factual. I waited about five minutes before a young man mid to late twenties walked in. He greeted me in English, he might have already known I was an American. He asked me where I was going with Skippy. I proceeded to tell him the story of Skippy (short version, very short).

After I finished, he asked to see my paperwork. I handed the paperwork over and told him about the error with Skippy's age. After a minute or two of perusing the CDC document, he turned it over and flipped it back again. He finally made eye contact with me and asked where is the USA stamp. I asked him what stamp he was referring to. He picked up a stamper from his desk and said this stamp as he held the stamper up.

I told him, "The USA did not stamp the paperwork because I have not landed in the USA yet."

He then stated the USA was supposed to stamp the document before I left the country. I told him I was unaware of a stamp prior to leaving, only the stamp when I arrived (which was a fib because I knew nothing about a stamp). He asked me what I was going to do with Skippy.

I answered him, "Have her become part of my family."

He said, "No, I don't mean if you get home. I meant since you do not have the stamp you need, I can't let the dog through to the next flight."

Now, I am worried. I told the man, "Listen I cannot fly all the way back to the US for a stamp and then come back to get the dog."

He stood up and walked over to a computer and typed something. He waited another minute staring at the screen and then walked back over to the desk. He stayed standing and looked down at me and said I have two choices.

One, take the dog back to Easter Island. Two, leave it here and Columbia will impound her.

I stood up to the five-foot-six-inch man and told him, "I would do neither of those two choices." I looked him in the eye and asked him, "There has to be another way?"

He went back to his computer typed a few things, stared at it again and walked back over to the desk. He said, "I have permission to use my stamp, if you are willing to pay 30 US dollars?"

I told him, "That would not be a problem." Then pulled out a fifty-dollar bill and handed it to him.

He told me he does not carry US currency.

I told him, "That's okay, I collect money from different countries [I do in fact.]"

He walked over to a file cabinet, stuck his hands inside and said from across the room he didn't have enough change.

I told him, "Hey listen, don't worry about it, just consider the extra twenty dollars a donation and can I still get the stamp?"

He walked back to the desk, put the fifty-dollar bill on the desk, turned the rabies vaccine paperwork over stamped it and said, "Here you go, amigo."

I took the paperwork, shook his grubby hand, and Skippy and I left the office.

After the fiasco with the immigration official, Skippy and I made our way to Avianca Airline ticket counter. I informed the clerk, Skippy was an ESA (Emotional Support Animal), and she will be flying in the cabin with me. The clerk asked me, "Why?"

SKIPPY'S RESCUE

She looked so tired, and I told her, "Skippy is in training and she is sedated for her safety." I handed the clerk Skippy's paperwork and the clerk took it to her supervisor.

The supervisor looked it over and said, "No problem."

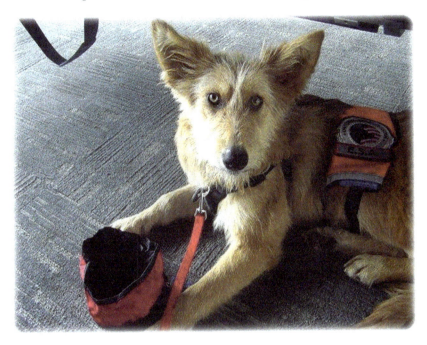

Going home

I asked the clerk if she would be able to move us to the first row behind first class because I am going to need leg room with Skippy. Again no problem, Skippy and I went through security without a hitch and made our way to the gate seating area. We took a seat away from others and waited for preboard. A young lady walking by us was nice enough to offer to get Skippy some water to drink.

I said, "That would be great!"

She came back and gave me the bottle of water. I asked her how much it was, and she said it was free. I thanked her again and got Skippy's little drinking bowl out. Good deeds are starting to come at us in bunches. I did not want her to drink a lot of water, just enough to quench her thirst.

Finally, preboard, we are going home! Skippy and I got to the entrance of the cabin, but there was no front row seating available for me. The attendant recognized this and flew in to action, she requested some people move here and others moved back here. Snap, snap, and we were all situated. A couple of children fawned over Skippy. Unfortunately, she was unresponsive to their kindness. Poor girl, wish she could enjoyed the smiles. Not to worry, she will bring us many smiles for many years to come.

The plane finished loading, and we are off the ground heading for home. I am so, so tired, yet unable to sleep because of the excitement of actually coming home with Skippy. Skippy slept most of the time we were on the airplane. She only started to become fidgety toward the end of the flight. We were five minutes from landing in Fort Lauderdale, Florida, when the captain made the call. "Weather delay, we will have to circle the airport until the weather clears up."

Ugh!

Finally, we get the all clear, and Skippy begins to fidget again this time she could not hold it. She let out a medicated smelling tinkle that could not be helped and it only disturbed one person that had to cover their nose. All other people on the plane felt badly for the little puppy. I had to take her out of the pee, so I put her on my lap. Not the smartest of moves, but hey, I can change out of my pants easier than trying to find a place to bathe Skippy.

It seems as if drama of some sort always follows us when it comes to our canine friends. The day we got Nocioni we had to make a huge decision. We would have to cancel our Galapagos Island vacation and lose some money if we took Nocioni home today. Or we could just leave Nocioni and take a chance of finding a dog like Nocioni when we get back. Needless to say, we lost quite a bit of money that day, but we gained a lifelong companion. Nocioni has been helping me get over the loss of Bubbs ever since, and he helped us when we lost Lobo for the second time. Yes, the second time. I had to take Nocioni to a town forty-five minutes from home to track Lobo. I made my intent with Lobo clear to Angelique when we rescued him. I wanted to rehabilitate Lobo and then find him a good home. We found a couple that were willing to take Lobo, they

SKIPPY'S RESCUE

understood his needs, and I felt they were a young couple that would be able to give Lobo many years of happiness.

The couple met Lobo a few times, Lobo took to the couple's child well, he displayed affection with both parents seemed like a great fit. The couple had Lobo for six to eight hours when I got the call Lobo slipped out of his harness and is loose running around town. I told the couple Noci and I would be there in the morning. Until then leave food out by the place you last saw Lobo, hopefully he will come around.

I didn't tell Angelique because I didn't want her to worry. I was confident Noci and I would find Lobo. The next morning, Noci and I headed out to find Lobo. I was hoping we could find him and bring him home before Angelique got off work. Spent the entire day tracking Lobo, and we just could not locate him. It got to the point in the day, I had to tell Angelique what was going on. Angelique offered to come to the area we were looking for Lobo and help.

I told her, "Stay home, I will be bringing Lobo home real soon."

Ten minutes after I hung up with Angelique, the young man that lost Lobo called me and told me he has spotted Lobo. I drove over to where he was and spotted Lobo. I got out of my car, opened my back door and called Lobo over. He took off the other way. I got back in my car and got ahead of him. Once out of the car, Nocioni and I ran up to Lobo, again he took off the other way. This time I had a plan, I let Noci go so he could chase Lobo. At the right time, I yelled out to Lobo, "LOBO!"

He stopped turned back around, saw Noci running his way and started running toward Noci. The two met like long lost lovers in a movie, they both stood up on their hind legs and pranced around for a bit.

In the middle of this I recalled Noci, and he came back to me and brought Lobo with him (so happy Noci has a good recall).

I told the young man, "Sorry, but Lobo is going with me." Lobo is going home.

America, what a country!

We worked our way through immigration, Officer Sanchez pulled me aside and said, "Okay, explain your dog?"

I proceeded to give him the short version of the story. "On vacation Easter Island, my wife fell in love with this dog, happy wife, happy life. I went back and got the dog. Here are the papers the CDC gave us to show when the CDC agent arrives."

Sanchez called his superior over and showed him the paperwork. His superior looked it over and told me, "You do not have to show your paperwork to anyone else, if someone ask, tell them US custom looked at it and said okay."

I sat around and waited for Skippy's crate to arrive, as I waited one thing stood out. US custom agents do not take crap. Every single person that took their cell phone out was reprimanded. I even tried to save a guest from doom, but he ignored me and got the "take it out again and it will belong to the USA" speech.

Love it! The crate finally arrived and Skippy and I were off to find domestic terminal Southwest Airlines!

We had to cut through the garage to get to the SWA terminal. Skippy got restless at one point and tried to move in her crate, when she did that, her and the crate tipped over. A man walking by was nice enough to stop and help me put her back on the luggage cart I rented. We made it to the SWA terminal without another accident. I can really smell the incident that Skippy had earlier, and I have to get out of these jeans. But, first I want to check her crate in. I waited in line at the ticket counter. When it was my turn I stepped up to the clerk and informed him, Skippy is an ESA dog in training and I need to check her crate in. I handed the gent my paperwork, he in turn showed the paperwork to his superior. The superior asked the clerk why he was showing him the paperwork, we don't question preboarding conditions.

Yippee, we get to preboard!

The clerk took the crate, and I was off to find a restroom. I found a couple of females sitting near the restroom. I approached them and explained my situation, I also told them that Skippy is on a sedative, and she wouldn't be a bother. They agreed to watch over her while I changed jeans. When I came out of the restroom, Skippy was in the same position I left her, poor girl she is so full of sleep. I thank the girls and picked Skippy up and headed to our gate. One more security checkpoint and we are free! As usual I carry Skippy through the detector, lay her down away from foot traffic, and walk through the detector again. We are cleared to head to our gate.

SKIPPY'S RESCUE

There are a lot of people in the gate area, looks like this is going to be a full flight. No matter, we are preboarding. A couple of kids walk by and ask to pet Skippy. The mother said that dog might bite the children. I told the mother Skippy is on sedatives and doesn't even know the children exist. She said okay, and the kids got to pet Skippy. After the children left Skippy and I were left alone. It's funny how you can tell who the people that are afraid of dogs are. They always make this weird face like, "How can you be that close to that animal?"

Because of the weather delay, we had to wait a little longer for the plane to get ready to take us home. We are finally on the fourth leg of our journey, and I am finding it hard to control my emotions. So many highs and lows in such a short span of time. Angelique told me before I left, God and I will move mountains. Well, I don't know about God but all these mountains we moved to get Skippy to this point has exhausted me. I'd like to think I could finally rest my eyes on the plane, but the excitement of finally coming home with Skippy will probably nullify that thought.

Skippy and Angelique together again

Preboard for SWA flight number 172 is beginning. I have two wheelchair people in front of me, and an elder lady with a surgical mask next to me. I am holding Skippy in my arms waiting for the operations' person to commence preboarding. A lady walked up to the operations person and asked a question I can clearly hear. "Is that dog getting on this plane?"

The op's person said, "Yes."

She then asked, "What about the people who are allergic to dogs?"

The op's person said they can elect to take a different flight or sit all the way in the back since the dog will be sitting in the front.

The lady than asked, "Why doesn't the dog take a different flight?"

The op's person says, "The dog isn't complaining about your illness."

Apparently, she did not like the answers to her questions because she walked away a bit disgusted. I, on the other hand, felt his answers were masterful!

This adventure with Skippy has only just begun. I see her doing many wonderful things the time she will be with us. Skippy could easily become a good citizen dog and visit nursing homes and hospitals. She could be an obstacle-course dog. She's already an Emotional Support Animal. There is one thing I will demand of her and that is she continues being a "freethinking" dog. A freethinking dog does not rely heavily on the humans of its pack. They go about their day with two paws in our home and two paws in nature. When in the home, they obey the house rules and live in unity with their human pack. While in nature, they stop and smell the air for signs of what is about. They listen for the field mouse rustling in the tall grass and watch the squirrel climb a tree. In the past, Noci, Lobo, and I would sit in the yard, and I would just watch the boys. I am constantly amazed at how much more in tune with nature they are. Smelling, hearing, and seeing things long before I am aware of—the cricket hopping along the grass.

Yes, I think Skippy is going to fit right in. I can't wait to watch the development of friendship these three will have. I know we will have some situations that will arise, but I am sure in the end, we will be one happy pack. I will continue to write about Skippy and her adventure as her life in America blossoms. Thank you so much for being part of this journey.

SKIPPY'S RESCUE

It's been a whirlwind since Skippy's arrival to her new country and home. She has made it through her introduction to the boys wonderfully. She also has become accustomed to the dreaded vet visit. Her first "real" car ride was a hoot. I slid the rear windows down a bit to give her some air in the back of my car. Apparently, it wasn't enough, so she stuck her whole head out the window, she really enjoys the ride. We had some issues with Skippy having a parasite from gnawing on tree nuts that the squirrels chewed on, but we got rid of that. Skippy's first weigh in was thirty-four pounds, not bad, but she really needs to put some weight on.

Angelique took Skippy to get her nails done (Angelique's nails), and Angelique made the mistake of leaving the back window open more than she should have. Fifteen minutes after arriving at the nail salon, a customer walked in and asked if anyone knew whose dog is sitting in front of a SUV in the parking lot.

3 amigos

Angelique got up and took a look. Sure enough, it was Skippy sitting in front of Angelique's SUV. Since then, we have begun to trust her more with her outside activities. She still wears a leash when she is outside, but it's a thirty-foot leash. Most of the time, she just drags it behind her. We step on the leash only when she strays a bit too far. Not sure what she would do if she was loose and saw a squirrel dash across the yard, we know she enjoys looking at the critters, but she hasn't made a mad sprint to catch the critters.

I really can't say enough good things about how Skippy has molded herself into our hearts. I think friendship comes natural to her. With Noci, she respects his age and rarely becomes physical with him (play fight), when they do get to playing, it's usually a grounded game. Noci's bad hips and knees prevent him from any tumbling, and I believe Skippy understands that. She even waits patiently at doors to allow Noci to go in first. With Lobo, it's a completely different story. These two go at it, its Katy bar the door time. I have always been of the opinion that Lobo lacked many social skills when he was with the hoarder before his rescue. At the age of four to five months when we rescued Lobo, you can tell something was missing. He lacked all phases of a happy dog. He mentally had issues with everything, especially men, children, and other dogs. Lobo will probably be a work in progress for the rest of his life. I believe Lobo would have been at Rainbow Bridge by now if Angelique didn't rescue him (twice). Skippy has really started removing a lot of that stigma from Lobo's past, she doesn't give him a minute to think about his past. She loves her brothers.

SKIPPY'S RESCUE

Skippy

Skippy's interaction with Angelique and I varies, she tends to relax more with Angelique and gets wound up with me. Angelique can watch TV in peace and Skippy and the boys only interrupt her when they are in need of something—mainly treats. With me, it's throwing the ball, play tug-of-war, and let-me-gnaw-on-your-hand.

The best part of this playfulness is when she has enough, Skippy nonchalantly takes the toy we are playing with jumps up on the couch and lies on the pillows above my head, and eventually, her head finds its way to my shoulder. Peace, till she decides to get down from the pillows and becomes my sixty-pound lap dog.

We recently had Skippy's DNA tested. I was very surprised at the results 25% German Shepard (that I knew) 25% White haired Swiss Shepard (never knew that breed existed) 12.5% Collie (must be where she gets her coat) 12.5% Rottweiler (surprised) 12.5% Boxer (Another surprised) 12.5% Mix breed. Absolutely no Terrier in her, guess I don't know dogs as well as I thought?

1st bath

1st day back found

New Friends

Resting

Skippy in snow

The Bullies

About the Author

Growing up in Chicago Heights, Illinois, could have been a daunting task for some children, but Ed had a way about him with animals that would make growing up a little easier for him. Beyond the acres of farmer's crops was a forest that Ed took a liking to. There, he would sit and watch the birds and squirrels climb and fly from tree to tree as he waited for his friends to arrive.

Ed's friends weren't the ordinary friends a young boy would have at this age, no, these friends were definitely different. A pack of feral dogs lived in the woods that Ed would visit and though the dogs were wild to most people, Ed called them his friends.

The pack of dogs would gather around Ed and wait for that morning's breakfast that Ed snuck out of his home. Ed would sit and toss morsels to the dogs and talk to them as if they understood every word he said. When the morsels were finish, Ed would get up and begin his trek back home only to be followed by the pack of dogs. Ed was unaware of the dangers a pack of dogs could present, he only knew the dogs as friends. Once Ed made it back to the edge of that year's crops, the dogs would vanish back into the forest assured Ed was back home safe.

Thus began Ed's extreme love for animals, especially dogs.

Printed in the USA
CPSIA information can be obtained
at www.ICGtesting.com
LVHW010854211123
764464LV00007BA/114